THE 7 HABITS OF HIGHLY EFFECTIVE PEOPLE

HABIT TRACKER

OTHER BOOKS IN THE 7 HABITS SERIES:

- *The 7 Habits of Highly Effective People*, including the 30th Anniversary Card Deck

- *The 7 Habits of Highly Effective People: Guided Journal*

- *The 7 Habits of Highly Effective Teens*, including the Card Deck

- *The 7 Habits of Highly Effective Teens: Guided Journal*

- *The 7 Habits of Highly Effective Teens on the Go: Wisdom for Teens to Build Confidence, Stay Positive, and Live an Effective Life*

- *The 7 Habits on the Go: Timeless Wisdom for a Rapidly Changing World*

- *7 Habits of Highly Effective Graduates*

THE 7 HABITS OF HIGHLY EFFECTIVE PEOPLE

HABIT TRACKER

INSPIRED BY THE WISDOM OF

STEPHEN R. COVEY

mango
PUBLISHING GROUP
CORAL GABLES

Table of Contents

Editors' Note

As editors of this book, we belong to different generations and different cultures. We grew up pledging allegiance to different countries, speaking different languages, and practicing different faiths and customs. While Annie enjoys the change of seasons and natural wonders that living near the Wasatch Mountains provides to someone who calls Salt Lake City her home, M.J. has grown accustomed to the noises of Florida, its mosquito bites and sweltering humidity, its crowded sidewalks and highways.

One thing we both have in common, though: we live very busy lives.

As the vice president of Books and Audio at FranklinCovey, Annie Oswald oversees the strategy and execution of book development. She's an expert at anything—and everything—related to international rights sales, licensing, and rights management, product and business development, partnership/relationship building, and IP marketing. When your role involves creating and managing the corporate strategy around thought leadership development and book development at the world's most trusted leadership company, your days in Salt Lake City start at dawn and can be long. And yet Annie has found a healthy, joyful work-life balance that drives productivity both in the office and at home. She frequently travels around the world with her husband and never misses out on quality time with her four daughters and her grandchildren. Annie's traveling feet hit the gym or the walk every morning.

On the East Coast., M.J. Fievre also wakes up before five o'clock. As the director of global editions and juvenile publishing at Mango, one of the nation's fastest-growing publishers, she has a tight schedule. Dividing her time between South and Central Florida, she manages the FranklinCovey imprint for Mango, commissions new books, runs both the children's division and the translation department, and serves as an in-house writer for the successful young adult brand, Badass Black Girl. Outside of Mango, she serves as a program coordinator for the Miami Book Fair and, because of her deep knowledge of several languages, as an expert witness for the criminal justice system. When she's not at work, M.J. is a caregiver for her mother and a Pilates enthusiast. She's active at her church and spends many evenings at Disney World and Universal Studios.

Because we're able to balance so many different facets of our lives, having attained this equilibrium where we equally prioritize the demands of our careers and those of our personal lives, we often get asked, "How do you do it?"

We are both quick to answer: "We practice the 7 Habits."

Dr. Stephen R. Covey's *The 7 Habits of Highly Effective People* was life-changing for us. Annie discovered this book when she went to work for the Covey Leadership Center just a few years after the book initially released. For M.J., *The 7 Habits* became a tool for her emotional survival in the late '90s. Growing up in an unstable and often violent environment in Port-au-Prince, Haiti, many times she almost surrendered to despair. Dr. Covey's teachings kept her grounded.

We welcomed the opportunity to edit this Habit Tracker together, not only because this tracker is inspired by a book that holds a deep meaning in both our lives, but also because our collaboration is the confirmation that the 7 Habits work—no matter who you are, where you come from, and what you've been through.

M.J. Fievre & Annie Oswald

How to Use This Tracker

The 7 Habits of Highly Effective People has captivated readers for over thirty years. It has transformed the lives of presidents, CEOs, educators, parents, and students. In short, millions of people of all ages and occupations have benefited from its lessons. With this Habit Tracker, the timeless wisdom and power of Stephen R. Covey's 7 Habits can transform you, too—one week at a time, in a stress-free way.

A habit tracker is a simple way to measure whether you adopted (or worked toward adopting) a habit. This habit tracker is designed for fifty-two weeks, a year. It includes a series of checklists that can serve as a form of meditation and growth; each checklist targets a specific habit. As time rolls by, these checklists become a record of your habit streak, allowing you to reflect and reset.

You can start this Habit Tracker anytime, but we encourage you to:

- Complete the self-assessment as you begin your Habit Tracker and again when you complete the fifty-two weeks.

- Follow the order of the checklists, as the 7 Habits are a continuum and build upon each other.

Throughout the pages, in addition to checklists, you will find quotes, lessons, and insights—all made available to help you invite change into your personal and professional life.

Nothing in this tracker is random—every checklist has been deliberately chosen to coax you into realizing things about yourself that you never knew or noticed before.

Here's to your highly effective life!

SELF-ASSESSMENT

7 Habits® Profile
Self-Scoring 7 Habits Profile

INSTRUCTIONS:

Read each statement and, using your best judgment, circle the number that indicates how well you perform in the following categories.

CATEGORY 1	Very Poor	Poor	Fair	Good	Very Good	Out-standing
1. I show kindness and consideration toward others.	1	2	3	4	5	6
2. I keep promises and honor commitments.	1	2	3	4	5	6
3. I do not speak negatively of others when they are not present.	1	2	3	4	5	6

Category Total: [ ]

CATEGORY 2						
4. I am able to maintain an appropriate balance among the various aspects of my life—work, family, friends, and so forth.	1	2	3	4	5	6
5. When working on task, I also keep in mind the concerns and needs of those I am working for.	1	2	3	4	5	6
6. I work hard at the things I do, but not in a manner that causes burnout.	1	2	3	4	5	6

Category Total: [ ]

CATEGORY 3

7. I am in control of my life.   1   2   3   4   5   6

8. I focus my efforts on things I can do something about rather than on things beyond my control.   1   2   3   4   5   6

9. I take responsibility for my moods and actions rather than blame others and circumstances.   1   2   3   4   5   6

Category Total: [ ]

CATEGORY 4

10. I know what I want to accomplish in life.   1   2   3   4   5   6

11. I organize and prepare in a way that reduces having to work in a crisis mode.   1   2   3   4   5   6

12. I begin each week with a clear plan of what I desire to accomplish.   1   2   3   4   5   6

Category Total: [ ]

CATEGORY 5

13. I am disciplined in carrying out plans (avoiding procrastination, time wasters, and so forth).   1   2   3   4   5   6

14. I do not allow the truly important activities of my life to get lost in the busy activities of my days.   1   2   3   4   5   6

15. The things I do everyday are meaningful and contribute to my overall goals in life.   1   2   3   4   5   6

Category Total: [ ]

CATEGORY 6

16. I care about the success of others as well as my own.   1   2   3   4   5   6

17. I cooperate with others.   1   2   3   4   5   6

18. When solving conflicts, I strive to find solutions that benefit all.   1   2   3   4   5   6

Category Total: [ ]

CATEGORY 7

	Very Poor	Poor	Fair	Good	Very Good	Out-standing
19. I am sensitive to the feelings of others.	1	2	3	4	5	6
20. I seek to understand the viewpoints of others.	1	2	3	4	5	6
21. When listening, I try to see things from the other person's point of view, not just my own.	1	2	3	4	5	6

Category Total: [ ]

CATEGORY 8

	Very Poor	Poor	Fair	Good	Very Good	Out-standing
22. I value and seek out the insights of others.	1	2	3	4	5	6
23. I am creative in searching for new and better ideas and solutions.	1	2	3	4	5	6
24. I encourage others to express their opinions.	1	2	3	4	5	6

Category Total: [ ]

CATEGORY 9

	Very Poor	Poor	Fair	Good	Very Good	Out-standing
25. I care for my physical heath and well being.	1	2	3	4	5	6
26. I strive to build and improve relationships with others.	1	2	3	4	5	6
27. I take time to find meaning and enjoyment in life.	1	2	3	4	5	6

Category Total: [ ]

CHARTING YOUR 7 HABITS EFFECTIVENESS

Total your points for each category in the Category Totals column. There are nine categories; the first two are the foundational habits of the 7 Habits, and the last seven are the 7 Habits.

After you have computed your category totals, mark each score in the grid below and graph your totals.

The higher your score, the more closely you are aligned with the 7 Habits principles. Where your score is lower than you would like, refer to the corresponding chapters (or modules) in *The 7 Habits of Highly Effective People* book to better understand how to increase your effectiveness in those habits.

CATEGORY TOTALS

	1	2	3	4	5	6	7	8	9
	Emotional Bank Account	Life Balance	Be Proactive	Begin with the End in Mind	Put First Things First	Think Win-Win	Seek First to Understand	Synergize	Sharpen the Saw
18 Out-standing									
15 Very Good									
12 Good									
9 Fair									
6 Poor									
3 Very Poor									

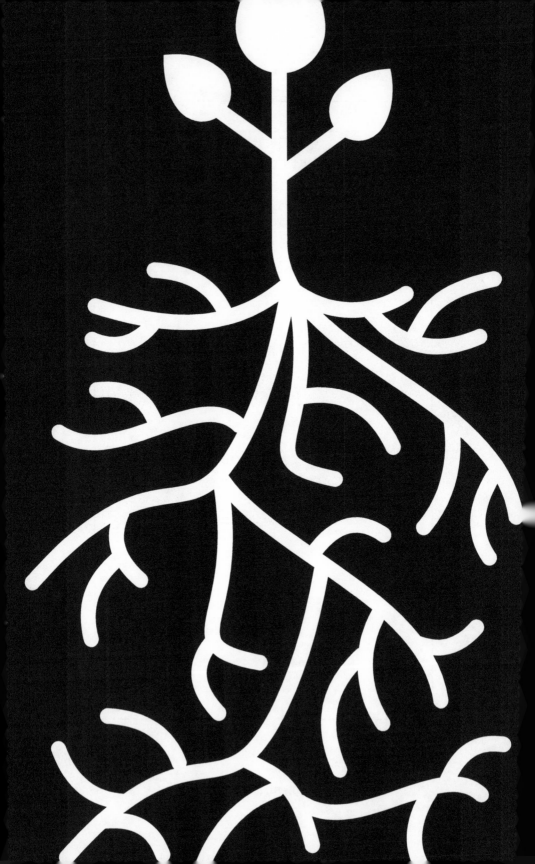

Introduction:
The 7 Habits

Habits are things we repeatedly do. But most of the time we are hardly aware that we have them. We mostly live life on autopilot. Some habits are effective, some are ineffective, and some don't matter.

Here are some examples of habits you may have: exercising regularly, blaming others, spending hours scrolling the internet, eating yogurt with a fork, showing respect for others, taking showers at night, and thinking negatively.

Depending on what they are, our habits can make us or break us. We become what we repeatedly do.

We all want to succeed. And one path to success is identifying the habits that can help us on our journey. The 7 Habits of Highly Effective People are:

1. Be Proactive™
2. Begin with the End in Mind™
3. Put First Things First™
4. Think Win-Win™
5. Seek First to Understand, Then to Be Understood™
6. Synergize™
7. Sharpen the Saw™

Habits 1, 2, and 3 focus on self-mastery and moving from **dependence** to **independence.** Habits 4, 5, and 6 focus on developing teamwork, collaboration, and communication skills and moving from independence to **interdependence.** Habit 7 is focused on continuous growth and improvement and embodies all the other habits.

IDENTIFY YOUR HABITS

Write three of your effective habits and three of your ineffective habits. Then write the results you get when you practice those habits.

Effective Habits	Results
1.	
2.	
3.	
Ineffective Habits	Results
1.	
2.	
3.	

Would you like to change any of the habits you listed? If so, which ones, and why?

_____

_____

_____

_____

Would you like to refine any of your effective habits? If so, which ones, and why?

_____

_____

_____

_____

THE MATURITY CONTINUUM

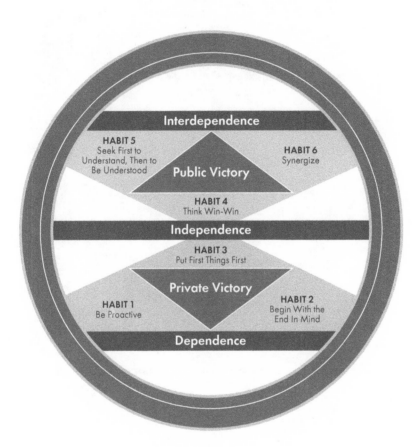

The 7 Habits create the Maturity Continuum, which is divided into three sequential states of development: dependence, independence, and interdependence.

Within the Maturity Continuum, **dependence** is the paradigm for *you*: You take care of me; you are responsible for my success; it's your fault.

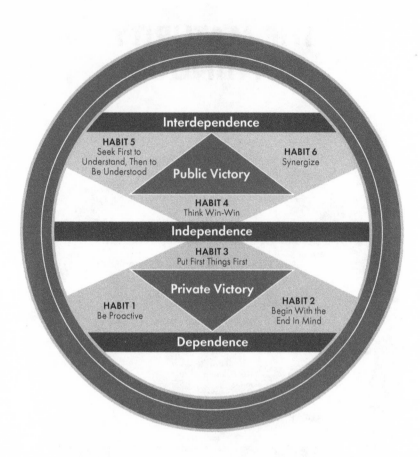

Independence is the paradigm for *I*: I am responsible; I can choose.

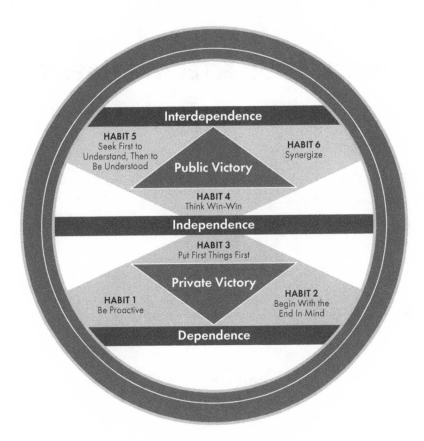

Interdependence is the paradigm for *we*: We can cooperate; we can do it; we can lift each other.

To gain true maturity, learn to value an **inside-out** approach to effectiveness centered on principles and character. Inside-out means that the change starts within yourself. It means you need to start from the foundation of your character and worldview; only then can you make lasting behavioral changes. Start examining and adjusting your character, motives, and how you see the world.

TRACK YOUR EFFECTIVE HABITS

In Week 2, you wrote three of your effective habits and three of your ineffective habits. You also wrote the results you get when you practice those habits.

This week, let's work on refining your effective habits. Can you track them for an entire week?

EFFECTIVE HABIT

DAYS

	Days
	M F
	T S
	W S
	T

	Days
	M F
	T S
	W S
	T

	Days
	M F
	T S
	W S
	T

HABIT 1:

Be Proactive
—the habit of choice

Proactivity means that as human beings, we are responsible for our own lives. Our behavior is a function of our decisions not our conditions. We have the responsibility to choose our responses. Proactive people do not blame circumstances, conditions, or conditioning for their behavior.

—**Stephen R. Covey**

When people are **proactive**, they pause to allow themselves to choose their responses based on principles and desired results. They often think about the day ahead and anticipate situations that might push their reactive buttons. This way, they can avoid reactive responses.

When people are **reactive**, they allow outside influences to control their responses.

Learn to pause between stimulus and response.

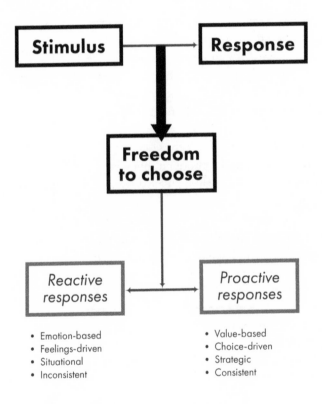

Consider your actions: What impact will they have? Who will be affected? Why could they be affected? How will it impact people/the situation and when?

TAKE A DEEP BREATH AND COUNT TO 10 (OR 100)

Checklist

THIS WEEK	DONE
1. In at least one situation, I paused to allow myself to carefully choose my response.	
2. In the morning, I visualized my day and decided what I could do to be proactive.	
3. I learned to identify my body's anger warning signs, and I thought about what the consequences might be if I lost control of my emotions.	
4. At least once, I used humor—not sarcastic, cutting, or unkind humor—to release tension.	
5. I took responsibility for my actions.	
6. I used "I" statements whenever I felt hurt.	
7. I chose my actions, attitudes, and moods.	

Weekly Reflections

YOU'RE IN CHARGE

Proactive people are the "creative force of their own lives"—they choose their way and take responsibility for the results. Reactive people see themselves as victims.

Language is a real indicator of the degree to which you are proactive. Using proactive language helps you feel more capable and empowers you to act. A proactive person uses proactive language (e.g., I can, I will, I prefer, etc.).

Using **reactive language** is a sure sign that you see yourself as a result of circumstances instead of as a proactive, self-reliant person. A reactive person uses reactive language (e.g., I can't, I have to, If only, etc.). Reactive people believe they are not responsible for what they say and do; they feel they have no choice.

For the next two weeks, whenever you feel yourself becoming reactive, summon one of the four endowments that make us uniquely human: self-awareness, conscience, imagination, and independent will. Try to use each of the four endowments for the day.

SELF-AWARENESS: I can stand apart from myself and observe my thoughts and actions.

CONSCIENCE: I can listen to my inner voice to know what's right from wrong.

INDEPENDENT WILL: I have the power to choose.

IMAGINATION: I can envision new possibilities.

HAVE A PROACTIVE DAY

Checklist

THIS WEEK	DONE
1. I made a list of everything that's going on in my life today that may affect my proactivity.	
2. I paid close attention to the language I used in my responses.	
3. I kept track of how often I hear reactive versus proactive language and the people using them.	
4. I stopped and thought before acting. I asked myself, "What's the right thing to do?"	
5. I was responsible for myself. Others did not "make" me feel a certain way—I chose to feel that way.	
6. When I caught myself being reactive, I tried the proactive approach instead.	
7. I used proactive language such as "I can," "I will," and "I prefer."	

Weekly Reflections

The 7 Habits of Highly Effective People: Habit Tracker

CONTINUE TAKING THE INITIATIVE

Checklist

THIS WEEK	DONE
1. I took initiative and solved a problem instead of panicking. I identified the problem, created a plan, and acted.	
2. I made good, responsible choices without being asked, even when no one was looking.	
3. I reached out to a colleague a few days before a deadline to offer support.	
4. I provided timely updates to my boss, team, clients, or whomever it may concern.	
5. I was active in meetings, giving suggestions, participating in brainstorming, sharing my opinions, and helping other team members.	
6. I did something kind for someone else.	
7. I asked trustworthy people to help me differentiate between venting, "dumping" (complaining excessively), and problem-solving.	

Weekly Reflections

The 7 Habits of Highly Effective People: Habit Tracker

CIRCLE OF INFLUENCE, CIRCLE OF CONCERN

Some things you can control (e.g., words, actions, and behaviors) and some other things are out of your control (e.g., past mistakes, family, coworkers, etc.).

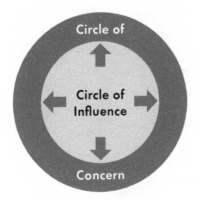

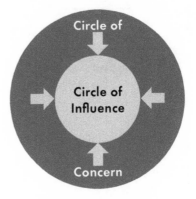

Proactive Focus
Positive energy enlarges
Circle of Influence

Reactive Focus
Negative energy reduces
Circle of Influence

Your **Circle of Concern** includes things you worry about but can't control. If you focus on it, you have less time and energy to spend on the things you *can* influence.

Your **Circle of Influence** includes those things you *can* affect directly. When you focus on it, you expand your knowledge and experience. As a result, your circle of influence grows.

Shrink your Circle of Concern. Expand your Circle of Influence.

SHRINK YOUR CIRCLE
OF CONCERN

Checklist

THIS WEEK	DONE
1. I created a list of things I can control and other things out of my control.	
2. Instead of fixating on what I can't control (e.g., "If I didn't live in this city"), I acknowledged my feelings and identified my fears. I then made a list of what I can control and concentrated on my influence.	
3. I reminded myself that life is uncertain— nothing is permanent, including setbacks.	
4. I wrote healthy affirmations and posted them where I could see them often.	
5. I changed my perspective and worked toward personal growth.	
6. I thought of a problem or opportunity I'm currently facing. I listed everything within my Circle of Concern and then let it go—burned it, shredded it, flushed it down the toilet.	

7. I considered "what *could* go wrong?" so that I could either accept the negatives (if they are beyond my control) or overcome them (if I can proactively make the negative a neutral or a positive).	

Weekly Reflections

CONTINUE EXPANDING YOUR CIRCLE OF INFLUENCE

Checklist

THIS WEEK	DONE
1. I made a list of everything I can control.	
2. Looking at my Circle of Influence, I determined an action I can take on each day this week to increase my influence.	
3. I fixed something that was broken or improved a relationship.	
4. I took action to improve my physical health and worked on a long-term plan.	
5. I didn't dwell on the mistakes from the past week but instead learned from them.	
6. I gathered all the required information before starting something new because I understand that the more I know, the more prepared I will be to make decisions I am confident about.	
7. I kept in mind that not all people thrive in all settings. I reflected on the possibility of changing my setting to ensure that I am successful.	

Weekly Reflections

BECOME A
TRANSITION PERSON

A **transition person** breaks a long pattern or tradition of unhealthy, abusive, or ineffective behaviors. They model positive behaviors and habits that strengthen and build up others.

This week, you'll focus on becoming a transition person by breaking some of the negative patterns that may have been passed on to you through your upbringing (abuse, addictions, bad habits, negative attitude, etc.). You'll reflect on how those patterns affect you and imagine what will happen if you no longer do those behaviors.

BREAK THE CYCLE

Checklist

THIS WEEK	DONE
1. I made a list of unhealthy behaviors I'd like to break, and I identified my triggers for these behaviors.	
2. I listed good reasons for breaking this negative pattern.	
3. I made a list of things I can do every day to break a negative pattern, including replacing the habit with a different one.	
4. I found an accountability partner.	
5. I made a list of things I can ask other people to do to help me change a negative pattern.	
6. I didn't wait for feedback—I actively sought it, showing a desire to learn and improve.	
7. I came up with a plan in case I revert to old habits.	

Weekly Reflections

_____

_____

_____

_____

_____

_____

_____

_____

_____

_____

_____

_____

_____

_____

The 7 Habits of Highly Effective People: Habit Tracker

Begin with the End in Mind

—the habit of vision

Habit 2 applies to many different circumstances and levels of life. The most fundamental application is to begin today with the image, picture, or paradigm of the end of your life as your frame of reference or the criterion by which everything else is examined. To begin with the end in mind means to start with a clear understanding of your destination. It means to know where you're going so that you better understand where you are now and so that the steps you take are always in the right direction.

—Stephen R. Covey

Habit 2 is the habit of personal vision. If you don't consciously visualize who you are and what you want in life, then you empower other people and circumstances to shape you and your life by default.

SEE THE BIG PICTURE

Checklist

THIS WEEK	DONE
1. I set goals for myself in areas that need improvement.	
2. Once I had clarity around where I am now and where I want to be, I started mapping out my journey and working to close the gaps between the two.	
3. I considered the support mechanisms I needed to get closer to one of my role models.	
4. I searched for the training and development needed to get me to where I wanted to be.	
5. I completed an aspirational profile.	
6. I started identifying the gaps between who I am and who I want to be.	
7. I shared my aspirations with my accountability partner.	

Weekly Reflections

The 7 Habits of Highly Effective People: Habit Tracker

YOUR MISSION STATEMENT

Being effective means putting forth effort in your most important relationships and responsibilities to define the legacy you want to leave.

Your mission statement defines your highest values and priorities. It's the end you have in mind for your life. It enables you to shape your future rather than letting it be shaped by other people or circumstances.

Your mission statement is not just for you. Your loved ones can benefit from knowing your goals, values, and vision.

CREATE YOUR MISSION STATEMENT

Checklist

THIS WEEK	DONE
1. I reflected on the legacy I want to leave; I wrote down how I'd want to be remembered by my friends, coworkers, and family members.	
2. I pondered the purpose of the goals I'm trying to achieve.	
3. I focused an hour each day on something that is an important part of my job and contributed to the organization's mission and vision.	
4. I said "no" to something that didn't serve my life purpose.	
5. I made an action plan.	
6. With a mentor, I discussed my goals and things I could do right now to be working toward those goals.	
7. I created a personal budget.	

Weekly Reflections

REFINE AND SHARE YOUR MISSION STATEMENT

Checklist

THIS WEEK	DONE
1. I visited http://www.franklincovey.com/msb/ and wrote the first draft of my personal mission statement.	
2. I reflected on the people in my life who have had the greatest influence for good, and I used this exercise to list the qualities of people who live according to their life mission.	
3. Today, I made a mental note or took a mental picture of something that inspired me.	
4. I shared my personal mission with someone I trust (a friend or family member) and I asked them to help me refine it.	
5. I chose not to compare myself to others and only compare myself to personal progress toward my goals.	
6. Before I acted, I pondered why I was about to do what I was about to do.	

7. I made decisions that led me to live my personal mission statement. I said "no" to the things that do not lead me toward living my personal mission statement.	

Weekly Reflections

BALANCE YOUR ROLES

In trying to fulfill all the key roles in your life, you can sometimes overemphasize one important role (often work-related) and get out of balance. As you focus on efficiency at work, for instance, you may sometimes overlook the people who matter.

In each of your roles, be mindful of every relationship's Emotional Bank Account. The EBA is very much like a checking account at a bank. You can make deposits and improve a relationship, or you can take withdrawals and weaken it. Deposits build and repair trust, while withdrawals break it down.

EBA WITHDRAWALS	EBA DEPOSITS
• Break promises	• Keep promises
• Keep to yourself	• Do small acts of kindness
• Gossip and break confidence	• Be loyal
• Don't listen	• Listen
• Be arrogant	• Say you're sorry
• Set false expectations	• Set clear expectations

In the next two weeks, you will balance your roles and rethink some of your relationships. True effectiveness comes from the impact you have on others.

BALANCE YOUR ROLES

Checklist

THIS WEEK	DONE
1. I wrote down all the roles I have in life and prioritized those roles.	
2. I reviewed these roles and limited my list to the top five most important roles.	
3. I pondered whether I'm getting absorbed in one role to the disadvantage of the others.	
4. I identified an important role that I might be neglecting.	
5. I thought about how the choices I make now will affect my future.	
6. I considered the positive or negative consequences of my actions before I acted.	
7. I wrote down my "end in mind" for an important relationship.	

CONTINUE BALANCING YOUR ROLES

Checklist

THIS WEEK	DONE
1. I balanced my self-care needs with the needs of an important relationship.	
2. I made consistent and frequent deposits into the emotional bank account of someone important to me.	
3. As a deposit into someone's emotional bank account, I sought first to understand what a deposit is to them. I listened empathically. I did not listen with the intent to reply.	
4. I actively chose when to talk things out and when to wait until we're both ready.	
5. In all my roles, I remained aware of boundaries. I made sure that physical touch/affection was mutually acceptable.	
6. I was respectful when offering support.	
7. I made a relationship a priority by being present.	

Weekly Reflections

Put First Things First

—the habit of prioritizing

Habits 1 and 2 are absolutely essential and prerequisites to Habit 3. You can't become principle-centered without first being aware of and developing your own proactive nature. You can't become principle-centered without a vision of and a focus on the unique contribution that is yours to make. But with that foundation, you can become principle-centered day in and day out, moment by moment, by living Habit 3—by practicing effective self-management.

—Stephen R. Covey

The 7 Habits of Highly Effective People: Habit Tracker

SET A GOAL

Habit 3 is the habit of personal and life management—living based upon your purpose, values, roles, and priorities. What are "first things"? First things are those things you find of most worth.

Your goals should reflect your deepest values, unique talents, and sense of mission. Effective goals give meaning and purpose to your everyday life and translate into daily activities.

SET A GOAL

Checklist

THIS WEEK	DONE
1. I blocked off uninterrupted time to plan.	
2. I set some goals for the week and created a weekly schedule.	
3. I set my top five priorities in life and verified that my weekly schedule reflected these priorities.	
4. I reflected on what's holding me back from going after the life I want.	
5. I started each day with a clear idea of what I wanted to achieve.	
6. I reflected on my greatest strength and how I've used it this week.	
7. I kept track of the steps I was taking to reach my goals.	

It's incredibly easy [...] to work harder and harder at climbing the ladder of success only to discover it's leaning against the wrong wall.

—**Stephen R. Covey**

DEFINE OUTCOME BEFORE YOU ACT

Checklist

THIS WEEK	DONE
1. I asked myself, "What one thing can I do that, if done regularly, would have a tremendous, positive impact on my life?"	
2. I wrote down five things that make me truly happy.	
3. I reflected on where I see myself in the future— in five years, in ten years, and at age eighty.	
4. In my planner, I scheduled the activities I needed to do to progress toward my goal.	
5. I created a list I can actually complete; my list is realistic, not ideal.	
6. I shared my daily and weekly plan with my accountability partner.	
7. I reviewed my plan and kept the focus on putting first things first.	

Weekly Reflections

USE YOUR TIME WISELY

The **Time Management Matrix** defines activities based on urgency and importance.

	URGENT	NOT URGENT
IMPORTANT	**Q1** NECESSITY Crises Emergency meetings Last-minute deadlines Pressing problems Unforeseen events	**Q2** EFFECTIVENESS Proactive work Important goals Creative thinking Planning and prevention Relationship building Learning and renewal Recreation
NOT IMPORTANT	**Q3** DISTRACTION Needless interruptions Unnecessary reports Irrelevant meetings Other people's minor issues Unimportant email, tasks, phone calls, status posts, etc.	**Q4** WASTE Trivial work Avoidance activities Excessive relaxation, television, gaming, Internet Time-wasters Gossip

Quadrant 1 is both urgent and important. It deals with the things that require immediate attention. Everyone has some Q1 activities in their lives, but some people are consumed by them.

When you are highly effective, you spend most of your time in **Quadrant 2** engaging in:

- Important goals
- Creative thinking
- Planning and preparing
- Building relationships
- Renewal and recreation

Quadrants 3 and 4 are **time wasters**—activities that steal time from you without giving anything back.

Effective people take time to plan every week before it begins. Your goals, roles, and Q2 activities are your "big rocks"—schedule them first and the "gravel" of less important tasks will fit around them.

Your character is revealed when you choose between your Q2 priorities and the pressures of the moment. You are effective when you align your choices with your mission, roles, and goals.

In the next weeks, you'll learn to prioritize for long-term success. As you spend more and more time in Quadrant 2, your Quadrant 1 will shrink naturally from the benefits of being better prepared, proactive, and properly rested.

DO IMPORTANT THINGS FIRST

Checklist

THIS WEEK	DONE
1. I learned about the four quadrants—Urgent versus Important.	
2. At the start of each day, I used the Time Management Matrix to estimate how many hours I'd spend in each quadrant. At the end of each day, I recorded how many hours I spent in each quadrant.	
3. I took my current to-do list and sorted all the activities into the appropriate quadrants.	
4. I started tracking my tasks and categorized them into the four quadrants.	
5. I put one Q2 (Extraordinary Productivity) at the top of my new to-do list.	
6. I filled the rest of the to-do list with everything I have in Q1 (Necessity).	
7. I identified the quadrant where I spend most of my time and reflected on the consequences and need for change.	

Weekly Reflections

USE YOUR TIME WISELY

Checklist

THIS WEEK	DONE
1. I chose an app (or paper planner) to plan my life.	
2. I prioritized my tasks and assigned due dates to all tasks.	
3. I looked at my to-do list often and stayed on top of my daily tasks.	
4. I revised my to-do list daily and said "no" to things I knew I should not or could not do.	
5. I reflected on a recent Q1 urgency that could have been prevented with preparation.	
6. I chose a Q2 activity that could significantly impact my life; I scheduled time to do it this week.	
7. At the end of the week, I conducted a review of the week, decided what needed improvement, and set my goals for the upcoming week.	

Weekly Reflections

PLAN FIRST, THEN ACT

Checklist

THIS WEEK	DONE
1. At the end of the week, I found a quiet place to plan for twenty to thirty minutes. I connected with my mission, roles, and goals.	
2. I set priorities, made a schedule, and followed my plan.	
3. I reflected on my roles and on the one or two most important things I can do in each role this week.	
4. I cleaned and organized my space.	
5. I planned my meals and went grocery shopping.	
6. I scheduled my social media usage to avoid time warps.	
7. I recharged my personal batteries; I focused on the positive, relaxed, and went to bed at a decent time.	

Weekly Reflections

PUT FIRST THINGS FIRST

Checklist

THIS WEEK	DONE
1. I reflected on what pulls me away from following through on my "big rocks."	
2. I made a list of time wasters and distractions and reflected on how I feel when I give in to pressures and neglect my true priorities.	
3. I formed bonds and strengthened relationships with my friends and family. For example, I spent time with my significant other "just because," or I read to my kids.	
4. I scheduled preventative maintenance on my home or car.	
5. I focused on self-renewing activities that inspire and uplift me, such as writing a book or producing meaningful works of art.	
6. I invested in my 401(k), savings account, CDs, or IRA.	
7. I considered/worked on a side business plan for additional income.	

Weekly Reflections

Private Victory to Public Victory

Most goals are challenging—otherwise, you would have accomplished them already! You can become frustrated if you procrastinate on a goal you truly want to accomplish.

Private Victory precedes Public Victory. Take a look back and survey the ground you've covered so far. Remember the Maturity Continuum. Identify where you are now. Habits 1, 2, and 3 have increased your self-respect and self-discipline and led you to a Private Victory of Independence.

After experiencing your Private Victory, Habits 4, 5, and 6 will lead you to a Public Victory of Interdependence where you will create habits of building rich, rewarding, enduring, and productive relationships.

For the next weeks, as you learn to keep your commitments to others, remember to also commit to kindness toward yourself. No negative self-talk. And celebrate every small win!

KEEP YOUR COMMITMENTS

Checklist

THIS WEEK	DONE
1. I took ownership. I didn't treat any of my commitments as a "maybe."	
2. I focused on Habits 1, 2, and 3 to better navigate my work and personal relationships.	
3. I was specific and realistic in making commitments, reflecting first on what I can truly commit to and making sure I was not over-committing myself.	
4. I took short-term steps. I did something to get me closer to living my personal mission, even if it was small.	
5. I monitored my progress by keeping a journal.	
6. I committed to kindness toward myself—no negative self-talk—and celebrated every small win!	
7. I thought of an important goal that I haven't made progress on. I considered the smallest possible action I could take toward that goal.	

Weekly Reflections

The 7 Habits of Highly Effective People: Habit Tracker

BUILD YOUR EMOTIONAL BANK ACCOUNT

The **Emotional Bank Account** symbolizes the amount of trust in a relationship. Deposits build and repair trust, while withdrawals break it down. Make sure you understand what a deposit is to each person.

Saying you're sorry when you've made a mistake or hurt someone can quickly restore an overdrawn Emotional Bank Account. It takes courage, but it can be done.

Everyone has been hurt at one time or another by someone else's thoughtless words or actions. It's important to apologize when you've done wrong; however, it's just as important to learn to forgive others. Sometimes, it's helpful to write a forgiveness letter to a person who wronged you. You don't have to send the letter but writing down your emotions gives them a place to live outside yourself and your body. You validate your emotions by breathing life into them.

BUILD YOUR EMOTIONAL BANK ACCOUNT

Checklist

THIS WEEK	DONE
1. I fulfilled a commitment that I had earlier made to someone.	
2. I identified three important relationships that might be in disrepair or are neglected. I listed three deposits I could make. I listed three withdrawals I need to avoid.	
3. I reflected on the steps I can take in the future to ensure a more positive balance and a stronger relationship.	
4. I apologized to someone I had wronged. I did not make excuses. I found out what I could do to repair the harm.	
5. I got a planner and blocked out time for my most important things and relationships (my "big rocks").	
6. Each day this week, I did one random act of kindness for a friend, colleague, or family member.	

7. I reflected on a relationship that will require many deposits to make up for the big withdrawal I made in the past. I made a plan for how I would restore trust.	

Weekly Reflections

HABIT 4:

Think Win-Win

—the habit of mutual benefit

Win-Win is a frame of mind and
heart that constantly seeks mutual
benefit in all human interactions. [...]
Win-Win sees life as a cooperative,
not a competitive arena.

—Stephen R. Covey

When you are highly effective, you value other people's wins equally to your own. You take time to identify both your wins and their wins. There is an even higher expression of win-win: Win-Win or No Deal. No Deal means that if you can't find a solution that would benefit us both, we agree to disagree. When you have No Deal as an option in your mind, you feel liberated because you do not need to manipulate people, push your agenda, or drive for what you want. You can be open. You can try to understand the deeper issues underlying their positions.

Win-win is an attitude toward life, a mental frame of mind that says, "I can win and so can you." It is not about you or me; it is about both of us. It begins with the belief that everyone is equal, no one is inferior or superior to anyone else, and no one needs to be the winner. Life is not all about competition, the way it may be in business, sports, and/or school.

If a relationship is not a win-win, is it worth maintaining? Pick an important relationship that could benefit from Win-Win thinking. Write down yours and the other person's wins. Don't know what they would consider a win? Ask!

EVERYONE CAN WIN

Think about your general attitude toward life. Is it based on win-lose, lose-win, lose-lose, or win-win? How is that attitude affecting you, your life, and your happiness?

For the next two weeks, whenever you get into two-sided situations, think about how both of you can benefit. Think, "How can I help this person?" and conversely, "How can this person help me?"

CONSIDER OTHER PEOPLE'S WINS AS WELL AS YOUR OWN

Checklist

THIS WEEK	DONE
1. I reflected on what relationships I'm less likely to think win-win.	
2. I pinpointed two areas of my life where I most struggle with comparisons. I pondered why I felt the need to compare myself and what I could do to minimize that need.	
3. I considered whether I'm in any lose-win or win-lose relationships.	
4. If I am in a win-lose situation, I outlined what I can do to make that relationship a win-win.	
5. I reflected on the steps I can take to prevent a lose-win relationship in the future.	
6. On all occasions, I asked, "What's in it for us?" instead of "What's in it for me?"	
7. I reflected on whether I am happy for the success of others. If not, I found an opportunity to congratulate someone for their accomplishments.	

Weekly Reflections: Week 23

Weekly Reflections: Week 24

The 7 Habits of Highly Effective People: Habit Tracker

CULTIVATE AN ABUNDANCE MENTALITY

When you have an **Abundance Mentality**, you are not threatened by others' success because you are secure in your self-worth.

A **Scarcity Mentality** causes you to compare, compete, and feel threatened by others instead of working *with* others for the biggest wins. The signs of a scarcity mindset may include believing that a situation is permanent (e.g., "I'll have to go without"); using thoughts and words of scarcity (e.g., "I don't have enough money" or "I can't do this"); being envious of others and having difficulty showing happiness for their success (e.g., "I don't think they're that great"); not being generous or finding it hard to share credit, recognition, power, and profit (e.g., "They can find their own way, just like I did"); and being overindulgent. With a scarcity mentality you may also struggle as a team player because differences in opinion are perceived as disloyalty.

For the next two weeks, reflect on where scarcity thinking is getting in the way of achieving your best results.

CULTIVATE AN ABUNDANCE MENTALITY

Checklist

THIS WEEK	DONE
1. I listed the areas of my life where I use a scarcity mentality and considered where this scarcity mentality might come from.	
2. I reflected on whether I truly believe that there is more than enough for everyone.	
3. Instead of making comparisons, I celebrated my and others' strengths.	
4. I shared resources with someone else, recognizing the unlimited possibilities around me.	
5. I asked myself, "How can I give more than expected? How can I serve others?"	
6. I became aware of my thoughts and watched what I said.	
7. When I hit a roadblock in a relationship, I reminded myself that "with people, slow is fast, and fast is slow." I gave the relationship time to think and process.	

Weekly Reflections

CONTINUE CULTIVATING AN ABUNDANCE MENTALITY

Checklist

THIS WEEK	DONE
1. I practiced gratitude.	
2. I cultivated and shared my passions, purpose, and knowledge.	
3. I freely offered to help others and nourish their energy.	
4. I focused on being confident, open-minded, flexible, and willing to learn.	
5. I thought big and embraced risks.	
6. I celebrated/recognized other people.	
7. I continued reflecting on the meaning of win-win.	

Weekly Reflections

BALANCE COURAGE AND CONSIDERATION

To be highly effective means to be courageous, willing, and able to speak your thoughts respectfully. It also means being considerate and willing to seek out and listen to others' thoughts and feelings with respect.

Are there relationships in which you lack courage or consideration? What price are you paying?

People who think win-win balance courage and consideration, and they commit to working to benefit both parties. They also recognize that public or private acknowledgment is a big win. You can build trust and strengthen your relationships when you generously share credit.

For the next few weeks, think about situations where you need to demonstrate more consideration. Focus not on interrupting but instead on acknowledging others and making sure everyone has a chance to be heard. Continue to think win-win.

The 7 Habits of Highly Effective People: Habit Tracker

BALANCE COURAGE AND CONSIDERATION

Checklist

THIS WEEK	DONE
1. I picked an issue I wanted to tackle with more courage. I wrote down the point I wanted to get across and visualized the conversation.	
2. I practiced a difficult conversation with someone I trust, using "I think" and "This is why" statements.	
3. I shared my ideas and opinions with confidence.	
4. I was clear about what I wanted to say.	
5. In conversations, I focused on facts, not emotions.	
6. In conversations, I paid attention to my body and verbal language.	
7. I waited for the appropriate opportunity to have a serious conversation.	

Weekly Reflections

The 7 Habits of Highly Effective People: Habit Tracker

CONTINUE BALANCING COURAGE AND CONSIDERATION

Checklist

THIS WEEK	DONE
1. I defined why my voice is important. I reminded myself: "There's a reason you're at the table."	
2. I developed my skills in a lower-risk environment to help me build confidence and credibility.	
3. I paused and breathed to maintain calm.	
4. I was an advocate for others.	
5. I balanced courage for getting what I want with consideration for what others want.	
6. I was empathic and courageous, saying what needed to be said with the other person's thoughts and feelings in mind.	
7. I cultivated an abundance mentality.	

Weekly Reflections

_____

_____

_____

_____

_____

_____

_____

_____

_____

_____

_____

EVERYONE CAN WIN

Checklist

THIS WEEK	DONE
1. I continued to think win-win.	
2. I chose a relationship that could benefit from win-win thinking. I wrote down what I think would be wins for that person (or asked them). I wrote down my wins and proposed a win-win agreement.	
3. When conflicts arose, I looked for third alternatives.	
4. I thought of an upcoming situation where I would be working on an agreement or solution with another person. I told the person I wanted to come to a solution that benefits each other and work together toward it.	
5. I thought about the people I interact with and identified someone who stands out as a great role model for thinking of win-win agreements. I learned from them.	
6. I thanked someone who has recently helped me accomplish something.	

7. I identified someone who deserves credit for something they've done or helped me accomplish. I privately or publicly acknowledged that person's contribution.	

Weekly Reflections

THINK WIN-WIN

Checklist

THIS WEEK	DONE
1. While thinking win-win, I stayed firm on values and flexible on the little stuff.	
2. I looked for and provided feedback—on ideas, approaches, behavior, and anything that could help us achieve better solutions, conclusions, and relationships.	
3. I identified the desired results (without dictating the methods to reach them) and deadlines; I described the positive and negative consequences of success or failure.	
4. I explained the parameters for achieving the results and warned of potential pitfalls as straightforwardly as possible; I listed the resources available—whether human, technical, organizational, or financial.	
5. I created accountability by setting standards and establishing check-ins.	
6. I tried to understand the issue from the other person's perspective, reiterating their concerns to fully understand their goals and concerns.	

7. I named the most important issues and concerns of both sides. I described these objectively and I figured out what results would be agreeable to both parties; I also determined a third option (beyond either side's proposition) that could achieve those results.

Weekly Reflections

Seek First to Understand, Then to Be Understood

—the habit of mutual understanding

When you really listen to another person from their point of view, and reflect back to them that understanding, it's like giving them emotional oxygen.

—Stephen R. Covey

PRACTICE EFFECTIVE COMMUNICATION

Listening with empathy means getting to the heart of what matters to the other person, whether you agree or not. When listening empathically, you listen with the intent to *understand*. You respond by reflecting feelings and words.

Empathic listening gets inside another person's frame of reference. You look out through it and see the world the way they do, understanding their paradigms and feelings. The essence of empathic listening is not agreeing with someone; it's fully, deeply understanding that person emotionally and intellectually. You're focused on receiving the deep communication of another human soul.

Empathic listening is, in and of itself, a tremendous deposit into the Emotional Bank Account. It's deeply therapeutic and healing because it gives a person psychological air—a human need second only to physical survival. This need for psychological air impacts communication in every area of life. Once you meet that vital need, you can focus on influencing or problem-solving.

Autobiographical listening is filtering what others say through your own story. Rather than focusing on the speaker, you're waiting to jump in with your perspective.

With empathic listening, instead of projecting your autobiography and assuming thoughts, feelings, motives, and interpretations, you're dealing with the reality inside another person's head and heart. You're listening to understand.

When emotions are high, focus on your intent. Don't worry about the correct response. Empathic listening requires a lifetime of practice.

Think of a time when someone listened to you with understanding and respect. How did you feel?

For the next few weeks, open your heart and practice empathic listening. You'll be surprised by what you learn.

LISTEN BEFORE YOU TALK

Checklist

THIS WEEK	DONE
1. I practiced empathic listening.	
2. I checked myself and tried not to interrupt, give advice, or judge.	
3. I worked on making people around me feel that I genuinely understand them.	
4. I asked people around me if they felt understood by me.	
5. I practiced listening for understanding by reflecting back the feelings of others and the content of their messages.	
6. I truly listened to those I love.	
7. In a conversation that was becoming emotional, I stopped and expressed to the other person that I would practice empathic listening.	

Weekly Reflections

The 7 Habits of Highly Effective People: Habit Tracker

PRACTICE EMPATHIC LISTENING

Checklist

THIS WEEK	DONE
1. This week, I continued practicing listening for understanding.	
2. I identified someone I often ignore or don't listen to closely and simply asked, "How's it going?" and then I took the time to listen.	
3. I recognize that I don't always have the right answers.	
4. I took the time to fully understand a situation, which gave me the most time to limit misunderstandings, gain clarity, and ask better questions.	
5. In addition to listening with my ears, I listened with my eyes and observed body language.	
6. I listened to other people's ideas and feelings and tried to see things from their viewpoints.	
7. I looked into the eyes of the person to whom I was listening.	

Seek First to Understand, Then to Be Understood

Weekly Reflections

The 7 Habits of Highly Effective People: Habit Tracker

AVOID AUTOBIOGRAPHICAL RESPONSES

Checklist

THIS WEEK	DONE
1. I continued listening for understanding.	
2. I listened only with the intent to truly understand, not the intent to respond.	
3. I listened without already forming a reply in my mind and overcame the urge to interrupt.	
4. I listened to others without interrupting, practicing the "ten second" rule.	
5. I checked my ego before listening to see the value in learning someone else's opinion, not just my own.	
6. I suspended my judgment of what was being shared and listened without bias.	
7. I asked clarifying questions and was able to sum up the conversation at intervals to show I was truly engaged in the conversation.	

Weekly Reflections

The 7 Habits of Highly Effective People: Habit Tracker

SEEK FIRST TO UNDERSTAND

Checklist

THIS WEEK	DONE
1. I continued practicing listening for understanding.	
2. When I had the opportunity to watch people communicate, I covered my ears for a few minutes and watched. I looked for communicated emotions that may not have come across in words alone.	
3. I took time to learn about other cultures.	
4. I listened to an audiobook and/or podcast that focused on effective communication.	
5. I practiced reflective listening.	
6. I asked relevant questions to show that I was listening.	
7. When the other person's communication was critical of me, I chose to only listen.	

Weekly Reflections

The 7 Habits of Highly Effective People: Habit Tracker

SEEK TO BE UNDERSTOOD

Seeking to be understood is the second half of effective communication. Once you are confident others feel understood, you can share your point of view with respect and clarity and expect to feel the same.

For the next few weeks, practice effective communication.

Remember that effective communication in the digital world requires the same intent and skills used in face-to-face communication. The challenge often lies in reading and relaying intent across media.

SEEK TO BE UNDERSTOOD

Checklist

THIS WEEK	DONE
1. I practiced speaking in a way that showed I understood the other person.	
2. I tried to clearly and calmly share my point of view.	
3. I actively prepared for an upcoming presentation or persuasive message I needed to give.	
4. I actively prepared for a difficult conversation that needed to take place.	
5. When imparting information on a new topic, I stayed away from details that might have distracted from the point I was trying to make.	
6. In all conversations, I gauged engagement and interest. I made sure that the people I was talking to were engaged and interested in what I had to say—it's the only way a message will be absorbed and retained.	
7. I shared my listening experience with someone I thought might benefit from my experience.	

Weekly Reflections

CONTINUE SEEKING TO BE UNDERSTOOD

Checklist

THIS WEEK	DONE
1. I clearly stated my intent. I was specific.	
2. I reflected on other people's feelings and words before expressing my own.	
3. I found other ways to "listen" with empathy during text, phone, and email conversations.	
4. I carefully read through the other person's communication. I took a breath and read through it again.	
5. After reading an uncomfortable or critical email, I wrote a response and let it sit for an hour or two. I came back later and saw if my words still reflected how I felt and how I wanted to say what I had to say.	
6. If emotions ran high in an email or text exchange, I asked a trusted colleague to review my response and give me feedback.	
7. I avoided trigger words and trigger punctuation in email communication.	

Weekly Reflections

PRACTICE EFFECTIVE COMMUNICATION

Checklist

THIS WEEK	DONE
1. I delivered my opinion to the intended audience with courage and consideration for their views.	
2. I chose the proper medium of communication.	
3. I streamlined and simplified, using concrete words and visual aids when necessary.	
4. I watched my body language. I remained aware of my body stance, hand placement, gestures, and facial expressions.	
5. I measured my voice by recording myself speaking and I played it back.	
6. I practiced speaking firmly and carefully chose my words so that my intent and message were appropriate.	
7. I practiced speaking in front of a mirror, the dog, or to people on the bus.	

Weekly Reflections

Synergize

—the habit of creative cooperation

When you communicate synergistically, you are simply opening your mind and heart and expressions to new possibilities, new alternatives, new options. You begin with the belief that parties involved will gain more insight, and that the excitement of that mutual learning and insight will create a momentum toward more and more insights, learnings, and growth.

—Stephen R. Covey

To put it simply, synergy means "two heads are better than one." Habit 6 is the habit of creative cooperation. It is teamwork, open-mindedness, and the adventure of finding new and better solutions to old problems.

Valuing differences is the foundation of synergy. You are effective when you value and embrace differences rather than reject or merely tolerate them. You see others' differences as strengths, not weaknesses.

Your paradigm is often that *you* are objective, but everyone else isn't. Effectiveness requires that you show humility and recognize the limitations of your perceptions.

In the next few weeks, you have a tremendous opportunity to grow from accepting others' experiences, points of view, and wisdom. Differences can be a source of learning rather than a source of conflict.

TOGETHER IS BETTER

Checklist

THIS WEEK	DONE
1. I questioned my "lone wolf" mentality and reflected on which relationships I tolerate differences rather than celebrate and value them.	
2. I chose a political or social issue I care about. Setting my personal views aside, I found a few people and discussed their views. I listened for understanding.	
3. I identified someone I disagreed with and made a list of their strengths.	
4. I learned about the unique strengths of the people I work and live with, and I reminded myself that there is great potential to learn from each other's strengths.	
5. I tried to walk in other people's shoes and pondered ways to value differences.	
6. In all interactions, I checked my motives and let go of the need to be right; instead, I reflected on what I could learn from those with whom I disagreed.	
7. I curiously and respectfully approached other people who were different from me and assumed that I could learn from them and them from me.	

Weekly Reflections

VALUE DIFFERENCES

Checklist

THIS WEEK	DONE
1. I contributed to a positive work environment that values respect and inclusion for everyone, regardless of differences.	
2. I discussed uncomfortable topics in private by meeting face to face in a neutral place.	
3. In all interactions, I strived to create the right atmosphere and contribute to a culture of communication; I was open to learning from different points of view or different ways of doing things.	
4. I listed some differences in my relationships (e.g., age, politics, style, religion, etc.) and wrote down what I could do to better value differences; I then invited and engaged people in respectful discussion, healthy debate, and exchange.	
5. To be sure my actions and words match, I tried to view my actions through the eyes of those who might not see things as I do.	
6. I confronted the deep-seated fears that might cause my aversion to those who think differently.	

7. I spent real time with those I disagree with and actively worked to find out which of the assumptions I hold are inaccurate.	

Weekly Reflections

_____

_____

_____

_____

_____

_____

_____

_____

_____

_____

CONTINUE VALUING DIFFERENCES

Checklist

THIS WEEK	DONE
1. I was patient, remembering the saying, "You can catch more flies with honey than with vinegar."	
2. I stayed calm and open and used "I" statements to avoid the blame game.	
3. I got to the point, clarifying the issue at hand to avoid confusion (a breeding ground for miscommunication).	
4. I supported my opinions with objective data.	
5. I remained open, looking inward and not assuming the other person was wrong; I sought to understand the other person's reality, doing my best to put myself in their shoes and understand where they were coming from, even if I didn't agree.	
6. I cultivated curiosity and asked questions, trying to find common ground, especially with shared values.	
7. I listened carefully and asked open-ended questions, making sure that my intention was not to change the other person's mind, humiliate them, or show them that they were wrong.	

Weekly Reflections

SYNERGIZE

Checklist

THIS WEEK	DONE
1. I showed genuine appreciation for the contributions that others make.	
2. I asked others what their strengths were and then utilized them to improve a project.	
3. I strategically thought about who's in my echo chamber and looked to connect with others of a different mindset.	
4. When hearing other people's opinions, I tried not to look for where I felt they were wrong but where they were right.	
5. I made a list of people who irritate me. Do they represent different views that could lead to synergy if I had greater intrinsic security and valued the difference?	
6. When I had a disagreement or confrontation with someone, I attempted to understand the concerns underlying that person's position.	
7. When I had a disagreement or confrontation, I addressed those concerns in a creative and mutually beneficial way.	

Weekly Reflections

REMOVE BARRIERS

You don't have to figure out all the answers by yourself. When you're dealing with a problem, **synergy** can bring to light ideas you would never have come up with on your own.

When you approach a problem with a willingness to synergize, you can come up with new ways to overcome it.

Synergy depends on a willingness to seek a **3rd Alternative**. More than just "my way" or "your way," a 3rd Alternative is a higher, better way. It's something that neither party would have, or could have, come up with on their own.

You get to a win-win agreement simply by asking, "How could we both win in this situation?" What you're looking for is a 3rd Alternative that's superior to anything you could create alone.

You are surrounded by the strengths of others but often don't tap into them.

REMOVE BARRIERS

Checklist

THIS WEEK	DONE
1. I pondered a problem that seems insurmountable when I think of facing it alone. I found someone (or a group) to talk to about the problem I'm facing and took the time to brainstorm.	
2. I sought out other people's ideas to solve problems because I know that, by teaming with others, we can create better solutions than any one of us alone.	
3. I reflected on the barriers that frequently prevent me from achieving my goals.	
4. I thought of a problem that would benefit from a 3rd Alternative and then researched some ideas.	
5. I became aware of what others were doing, applauded their efforts, acknowledged their successes, and encouraged them in their pursuits.	
6. I noted when I became defensive and asked for feedback on my behavior.	
7. I made a special effort to collaborate with others.	

Weekly Reflections

The 7 Habits of Highly Effective People: Habit Tracker

CONTINUE REMOVING BARRIERS

Checklist

THIS WEEK	DONE
1. I thought about a goal I'm working on. I identified where and why I was stuck. I found someone to help me brainstorm ways to overcome those obstacles.	
2. I found someone who challenges and inspires me and spent time with them.	
3. I made a list of things I can do to take greater advantage of the strengths of others in my life.	
4. I listed the strengths of all my closest friends, family, and colleagues and matched these strengths to a challenge I was facing.	
5. When I noticed I've been working independently on a project, I took a moment and shared my work (even if it's still in progress) with someone else. I asked for their opinion. I listened to their opinion with the intent to understand, not to respond.	
6. As I worked with a colleague on a new project, we agreed to explore and be open to new possibilities.	

7. I recognized the feelings that accompany a 3rd Alternative: new energy and excitement, a sense that the relationship has been transformed, and the conviction that we ended with an idea better than either could have come up with alone.

Weekly Reflections

HABIT 7:

Sharpen the Saw
—the habit of renewal

Habit 7 is preserving and enhancing the greatest asset you have—you. It's renewing the four dimensions of your nature—physical, spiritual, mental, and social/emotional. Habit 7 surrounds the other habits on the maturity continuum because it is the habit that makes all the others possible.

—Stephen R. Covey

THE 4 DIMENSIONS

Time routinely spent each day renewing one's body, mind, heart, and spirit is key to developing all of the 7 Habits.

- **Physical:** This involves caring for your physical body—a healthy diet, sufficient rest, and regular exercise.

- **Mental:** As soon as people leave school, many let their minds atrophy. But continued learning is vital to mental renewal. You learn in many ways and places, not just at school.

- **Spiritual:** This is a private area of life and a supremely important one. It draws on sources that inspire and uplift you.

- **Social/Emotional:** Your emotional life is primarily (but not exclusively) developed through your relationships with other people.

In the next few weeks, spend time each day renewing your body, mind, heart, and spirit.

FOCUS ON SELF-RENEWAL

Checklist

THIS WEEK	DONE
1. I wrote in my journal my current routine for daily renewal and reflected on where I can improve.	
2. I adopted a mentality of constant self-renewal and a lifetime of learning.	
3. I actively pondered the steps I can take now to grow for tomorrow.	
4. I changed my current approach to self-renewal by realigning my goals into a more holistic approach to life.	
5. I made a list of activities that would help me keep in good physical shape, fit my lifestyle, and could be enjoyed over time.	
6. I made a similar list of renewing activities in my spiritual and mental dimensions.	
7. In my social-emotional area, I listed relationships I would like to improve.	

Weekly Reflections

CONTINUE BUILDING YOUR CAPACITY

Checklist

THIS WEEK	DONE
1. I researched ways I could improve my strength and resilience.	
2. I chose one way to build my physical capacity this week. For example, I began by adding in a twenty-minute walk every day.	
3. I chose one way to build my spiritual capacity. For example, I spent time in nature, listened to or created music, volunteered in my community, or participated in religious traditions.	
4. I centered on my values, reflecting on what inspires and lifts me.	
5. I refined my personal mission statement.	
6. I spent time with family and friends.	
7. I combined physical and spiritual goals by going for a walk in nature and deliberately and internally expressed gratitude for the things I encountered on my walk.	

Weekly Reflections

CONTINUE BUILDING YOUR CAPACITY

Checklist

THIS WEEK	DONE
1. I pondered ways to build my social/ emotional capacity.	
2. I invited a friend I hadn't heard from lately to dinner.	
3. I planned and participated in a family game night.	
4. I helped everyone at home set a goal for the week.	
5. I read together with a family member.	
6. I forgave someone.	
7. I reflected on what I need to forgive myself for.	
8. I took time to find meaningful ways to help others.	

Weekly Reflections

TAKE TIME FOR YOURSELF

Renewal is a Quadrant 2 activity. We must be proactive to make it happen.

In the next few weeks, remember to tame technology. Your devices can be the ultimate sources of urgencies. You may feel productive responding to every message, but mostly, you're letting yourself be distracted.

TAKE TIME FOR YOURSELF

Checklist

THIS WEEK	DONE
1. I read a good book, listened to an uplifting podcast, and/or watched a TED Talk.	
2. I took a short nap; took a hot relaxing bath with essential oils; meditated or listened to relaxing music; practiced a breathing technique.	
3. I prepared a healthy and nourishing meal, made my own juice, or drank a cup of herbal tea.	
4. I put on some upbeat music and danced.	
5. I watched funny cat videos or played with my pet.	
6. I called a friend to laugh, not vent; I called, texted, or emailed a family member to catch up.	
7. I turned off my phone.	

Weekly Reflections

The 7 Habits of Highly Effective People: Habit Tracker

CONTINUE TAKING TIME FOR YOURSELF

Checklist

THIS WEEK	DONE
1. I practiced deep breathing exercises.	
2. I went for a walk or a swim or did a high endurance workout or a peaceful yoga exercise.	
3. I checked out some motivational quotes or wrote some positive affirmations.	
4. I journaled or relaxed with an adult coloring book.	
5. I handwrote a positive message to my future self.	
6. I planned my dream vacation.	
7. I wrote letters of gratitude to important people in my life.	

Weekly Reflections

TAME TECHNOLOGY

Checklist

THIS WEEK	DONE
1. I pondered whether I've been using technology at the expense of my most important goals and relationships.	
2. I did one thing to reduce distractions from technology: I turned off alerts, I turned off my devices while working on my "big rocks," or I blocked out times when I don't check social media feeds.	
3. I made (and kept) a promise never to let my device interrupt a conversation.	
4. I kept technology out of the bedroom.	
5. I used an old-fashioned alarm clock so that my phone was not the first thing I reached for in the morning.	
6. I scheduled gadget-free periods each day. I completely turned off my phone during that time.	
7. I downloaded apps to help me better manage my finances. I added the relevant information to the app to do online budgeting.	

Weekly Reflections

The 7 Habits of Highly Effective People: Habit Tracker

CONTINUE TAMING TECHNOLOGY

Checklist

THIS WEEK	DONE
1. I continued to tame technology—I deleted unnecessary apps and organized apps under categories.	
2. I was 100 percent present in conversations—I turned off my phone and shut down the screen.	
3. I did a week-long tech detox. I abstained from personal social media for a full week.	
4. I unsubscribed from unnecessary accounts or email lists, muted or unfollowed people, and left groups.	
5. I scheduled time daily to look at and respond to emails.	
6. I filled my days so that there was no spare time to surf the net.	
7. I hid or deleted any haters or energy-suckers from my social media accounts.	

Weekly Reflections

SHARPEN THE SAW

Checklist

THIS WEEK	DONE
1. I reflected on the urgencies crowding out my renewal time, such as incoming emails, a colleague's roller-coaster emotional life, office gossip, etc.	
2. I took thirty minutes for myself; I found a stress buster and reflected afterward on how it made me feel.	
3. I wrote a list of things I'm grateful for.	
4. I dreamed a little and created a list of goals that covered the four dimensions of life.	
5. I made a list of things, people, places, and events that make me feel happy to be alive and reflected on how I can add more of those into my life.	
6. I showed compassion toward myself.	
7. I recorded my goal in my calendar and made time to sharpen the saw.	

Weekly Reflections

The 7 Habits of Highly Effective People: Habit Tracker

SELF-ASSESSMENT

Redo the self-assessment and compare it to the earlier self-assessment.

7 Habits® Profile
Self-Scoring 7 Habits Profile

INSTRUCTIONS:

Read each statement and, using your best judgment, circle the number that indicates how well you perform in the following categories.

CATEGORY 1

	Very Poor	Poor	Fair	Good	Very Good	Out-standing
1. I show kindness and consideration toward others.	1	2	3	4	5	6
2. I keep promises and honor commitments.	1	2	3	4	5	6
3. I do not speak negatively of others when they are not present.	1	2	3	4	5	6

Category Total: ☐

CATEGORY 2

4. I am able to maintain an appropriate balance among the various aspects of my life—work, family, friends, and so forth.	1	2	3	4	5	6
5. When working on task, I also keep in mind the concerns and needs of those I am working for.	1	2	3	4	5	6
6. I work hard at the things I do, but not in a manner that causes burnout.	1	2	3	4	5	6

Category Total: ☐

CATEGORY 3

7.	I am in control of my life.	1	2	3	4	5	6
8.	I focus my efforts on things I can do something about rather than on things beyond my control.	1	2	3	4	5	6
9.	I take responsibility for my moods and actions rather than blame others and circumstances.	1	2	3	4	5	6

Category Total: [ ]

CATEGORY 4

10.	I know what I want to accomplish in life.	1	2	3	4	5	6
11.	I organize and prepare in a way that reduces having to work in a crisis mode.	1	2	3	4	5	6
12.	I begin each week with a clear plan of what I desire to accomplish.	1	2	3	4	5	6

Category Total: [ ]

CATEGORY 5

13.	I am disciplined in carrying out plans (avoiding procrastination, time wasters, and so forth).	1	2	3	4	5	6
14.	I do not allow the truly important activities of my life to get lost in the busy activities of my days.	1	2	3	4	5	6
15.	The things I do everyday are meaningful and contribute to my overall goals in life.	1	2	3	4	5	6

Category Total: [ ]

CATEGORY 6

16.	I care about the success of others as well as my own.	1	2	3	4	5	6
17.	I cooperate with others.	1	2	3	4	5	6
18.	When solving conflicts, I strive to find solutions that benefit all.	1	2	3	4	5	6

Category Total: [ ]

CATEGORY 7	Very Poor	Poor	Fair	Good	Very Good	Out-standing
19. I am sensitive to the feelings of others.	1	2	3	4	5	6
20. I seek to understand the viewpoints of others.	1	2	3	4	5	6
21. When listening, I try to see things from the other person's point of view, not just my own.	1	2	3	4	5	6

Category Total: ☐

CATEGORY 8

22. I value and seek out the insights of others.	1	2	3	4	5	6
23. I am creative in searching for new and better ideas and solutions.	1	2	3	4	5	6
24. I encourage others to express their opinions.	1	2	3	4	5	6

Category Total: ☐

CATEGORY 9

25. I care for my physical heath and well being.	1	2	3	4	5	6
26. I strive to build and improve relationships with others.	1	2	3	4	5	6
27. I take time to find meaning and enjoyment in life.	1	2	3	4	5	6

Category Total: ☐

CHARTING YOUR 7 HABITS EFFECTIVENESS

Total your points for each category in the Category Totals column. There are nine categories; the first two are the foundational habits of the 7 Habits, and the last seven are the 7 Habits.

After you have computed your category totals, mark each score in the grid below and graph your totals.

The higher your score, the more closely you are aligned with the 7 Habits principles. Where your score is lower than you would like, refer to the corresponding chapters (or modules) in The 7 Habits of Highly Effective People book to better understand how to increase your effectiveness in those habits.

CATEGORY TOTALS

	1	2	3	4	5	6	7	8	9
	Emotional Bank Account	Life Balance	Be Proactive	Begin with the End in Mind	Put First Things First	Think Win-Win	Seek First to Understand	Synergize	Sharpen the Saw
18 Out-standing									
15 Very Good									
12 Good									
9 Fair									
6 Poor									
3 Very Poor									

There Is More

The 7 Habits of Highly Effective People is one of the most inspiring and impactful books ever written. We hope that, with this journal, you've enjoyed and learned critical lessons about the habits of highly effective and successful people, and that these lessons will continue to enrich your life experiences.

You can learn more about the timeless wisdom and principles of Stephen R. Covey by purchasing *The 7 Habits of Highly Effective People*, available in all formats, including a highly readable and understandable infographics format.

Best wishes on becoming the best version of you!

About Stephen R. Covey

Stephen R. Covey was an internationally respected leadership authority, family expert, teacher, organizational consultant, and author who dedicated his life to teaching principle-centered living and leadership to build both families and organizations. He earned an MBA from Harvard University and a doctorate from Brigham Young University, where he was a professor of organizational behavior and business management and also served as director of university relations and assistant to the president.

Dr. Covey was the author of several acclaimed books, including the international bestseller *The 7 Habits of Highly Effective People*, which was named the #1 Most Influential Business Book of the Twentieth Century and one of the top ten most influential management books ever. It has sold more than 20 million copies in thirty-eight languages throughout the world. Other bestsellers include First Things First, Principle-Centered Leadership, and *The 7 Habits of Highly Effective Families*, bringing the combined total to more than 25 million books sold.

As a father of nine and grandfather of forty-three, he earned the 2003 Fatherhood Award from the National Fatherhood Initiative, which he said was the most meaningful award he ever received. Other awards given to Dr. Covey include the Thomas More College Medallion for continuing service to humanity, Speaker of the Year in 1999, the Sikh's 1998 International Man of Peace Award, the 1994 International Entrepreneur of the Year Award, and the National Entrepreneur of the Year Lifetime Achievement Award for Entrepreneurial Leadership. Dr. Covey was recognized as one of

TIME magazine's 25 Most Influential Americans and received seven honorary doctorate degrees.

Dr. Covey was the cofounder and vice chairman of FranklinCovey Company, the leading global professional services firm, with offices in 123 countries. They share Dr. Covey's vision, discipline, and passion to inspire, lift, and provide tools for change and growth of individuals and organizations throughout the world.

About the Editors

Born in Haiti, **Michele Jessica "M.J." Fievre** is a longtime educator and writer who has been praised as a model of efficiency and effectiveness. She helps others write their way through trauma, build community, and create social change. She works with veterans, disenfranchised youth, cancer patients and survivors, victims of domestic and sexual violence, minorities, the elderly, those with chronic illness or going through transition, and any underserved population in need of writing as a form of therapy—even if they don't realize that they need writing or therapy. She's the author of the two bestselling series *Badass Black Girl* and *Bold and Black*.

M.J. lives in Winter Garden, Florida, with her husband, artist Thomas B. Logan.

★ ★ ★

Annie Oswald is the Vice President of Books & Audio of FranklinCovey Company—the company that brings you several global bestselling self-help, business, motivational, and education books.

Annie has served at FranklinCovey for over thirty years and has been an integral part of the conception and development of global bestsellers, including *The 7 Habits, The 7 Habits of Highly Effective Teens, The 4 Disciplines of Execution, The 7 Habits of Happy Kids*, and many, many more. Her favorite part of her job is creating win–win relationships with international publishers.

Annie and her husband live in the Rocky Mountains of Utah and they are the proud parents of four daughters. She graduated with a degree in English and communications, she's taught the 7 Habits at the local community university, and has taught 7 Habits content around the world.

Annie encourages everyone to seek life effectiveness through living the principles of the 7 Habits.

**FranklinCovey**

FranklinCovey is the most trusted leadership company in the world, with operations in over 160 countries. We transform organizations by partnering with our clients to build leaders, teams, and cultures that get breakthrough results through collective action, which leads to a more engaging work experience for their people.

Available through the FranklinCovey All Access Pass®, our best-in-class content, solutions, experts, technology, and metrics seamlessly integrate to ensure lasting behavior change at scale.

This approach to leadership and organizational change has been tested and refined by working with tens of thousands of teams and organizations over the past 30 years.

To learn more, visit
FRANKLINCOVEY.COM.

FranklinCovey
All Access Pass

The FranklinCovey All Access Pass® provides unlimited access to our best-in-class content and solutions, allowing you to expand your reach, achieve your business objectives, and sustainably impact performance across your organization.

AS A PASSHOLDER, YOU CAN:

- Access FranklinCovey's world-class content, whenever and wherever you need it, including *The 7 Habits of Highly Effective People®: Signature Edition 4.0*, Leading at the *Speed of Trust®*, *The 5 Choices to Extraordinary Productivity®*, and *Unconscious Bias: Understanding Bias to Unleash Potential™*.

- Certify your internal facilitators to teach our content, deploy FranklinCovey consultants, or use digital content to reach your learners with the behavior-changing content you require.

- Have access to a certified implementation specialist who will help design Impact Journeys for behavior change.

- Organize FranklinCovey content around your specific business-related needs.

- Build a common learning experience throughout your entire global organization with our core-content areas localized into 23 languages.

Join thousands of organizations using the All Access Pass to implement strategy, close operational gaps, increase sales, drive customer loyalty, and improve employee engagement.

To learn more, visit
FRANKLINCOVEY.COM or call **1-888-868-1776**.

CHANGE
How to Turn Uncertainty Into Opportunity™

FranklinCovey
ALL ACCESS PASS™

Change happens all the time, whether we choose it or it chooses us.

Yet, when faced with change, many organizations primarily focus on the process. Successful change takes more than that—**it's your people who make change happen**. And as people, we're wired to react to change to survive, which can make change feel difficult or threatening. Successful leaders engage their people in change, making it feel less uncertain and more like an opportunity.

Introducing *Change: How to Turn Uncertainty Into Opportunity*

When we recognize that change follows a predictable pattern, we can learn to manage our reactions and understand how to navigate change, both functionally and emotionally. This allows us to consciously determine how to best move forward—even in the most challenging stages.

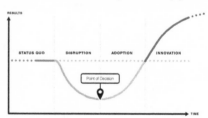

Change: How to Turn Uncertainty Into Opportunity helps individuals and leaders learn how to successfully navigate any workplace change to improve results.

To learn more about how FranklinCovey's
Change: How to Turn Uncertainty Into Opportunity
can support your team and organization, visit

franklincovey.com/leadership/navigate-change

Read More
FROM THE FRANKLINCOVEY LIBRARY

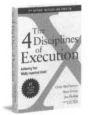

MORE THAN 50 MILLION COPIES SOLD

Learn more about how to develop yourself personally, lead your team, or transform your organization with these bestselling books, by visiting **7habitsstore.com**.

FRANKLINCOVEY
ONLEADERSHIP
WITH
SCOTT MILLER

Join *On Leadership* host Scott Miller for weekly interviews with thought leaders, bestselling authors, and world-renowned experts on the topics of organizational culture, leadership development, execution, and personal productivity.

FEATURED INTERVIEWS INCLUDE:

CHRIS McCHESNEY
THE 4 DISCIPLINES OF
EXECUTION

SUSAN DAVID
EMOTIONAL AGILITY

KIM SCOTT
RADICAL CANDOR

DANIEL PINK
WHEN

SETH GODIN
THE DIP, LINCHPIN, PURPLE COW

NELY GALÁN
SELF MADE

LIZ WISEMAN
MULTIPLIERS / IMPACT PLAYERS

GUY KAWASAKI
WISE GUY

STEPHEN M. R. COVEY
THE SPEED OF TRUST

ARIANNA HUFFINGTON
THRIVE NOW

NANCY DUARTE
DATA STORY, SLIDE:OLOGY

STEPHANIE McMAHON
CEO, WWE

DEEPAK CHOPRA
ABUNDANCE

ANNE CHOW
CEO, AT&T BUSINESS

GENERAL STANLEY
McCHRYSTAL
LEADERS: MYTH AND REALITY

MATTHEW
McCONAUGHEY
GREENLIGHTS

Subscribe to FranklinCovey's *On Leadership* to receive weekly videos, tools, articles, and podcasts at

FRANKLINCOVEY.COM/ONLEADERSHIP.

CPSIA information can be obtained
at www.ICGtesting.com
Printed in the USA
LVHW011804191122
733604LV00002B/269